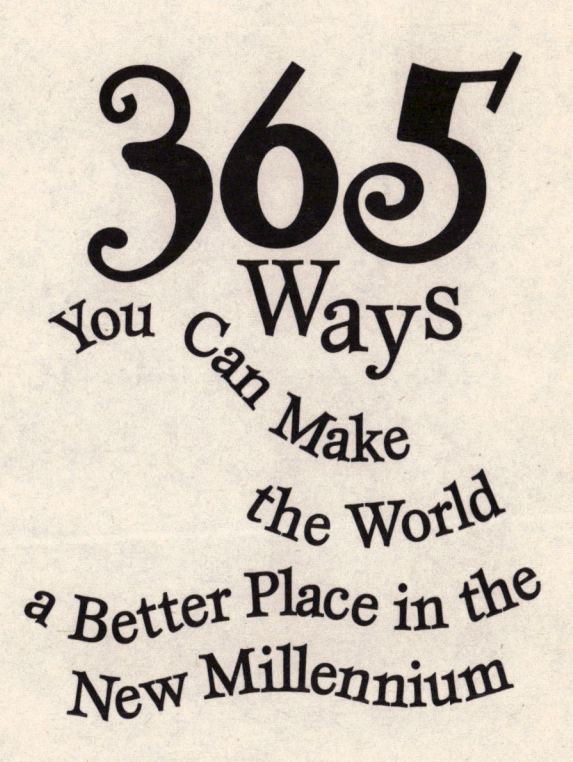

365 Ways You Can Make the World a Better Place in the New Millennium

Contest-winning ideas by kids for kids!

365 Ways You Can Make the World a Better Place in the New Millennium

Contest-winning ideas by kids for kids!

Edited by Peggy Gavan

Text copyright © 1999 by Troll Communications L.L.C.

All rights reserved. No part of this book may be reproduced or utilized in any form or by any means, electronic or mechanical, including photocopying, recording, or by any information storage and retrieval system, without written permission from the publisher.

Printed in the United States of America.

10 9 8 7 6 5 4 3 2 1

WHAT COULD YOU DO TO MAKE THE WORLD A BETTER PLACE IN THE NEW MILLENNIUM?

That's the question we asked kids across America in our *Millennium Mania* contest. The response was tremendous! Thousands of students in grades K-9 gave us their best ideas for improving our world—from helping the environment and donating to charity to inventing great technology to make everyone's lives easier and more exciting.

We took the very best ideas—innovative, sensitive, humorous, or thought provoking—and compiled them in this book.

Thank you to all the students who entered the contest and to all the teachers who encouraged them. We hope you will be inspired to apply some of these wonderful suggestions to your own life, to make every day of the new millennium better than the next!

Sincerely,

Peggy Gavan
Editor

LOOK ON THE BRIGHT SIDE

1 I can make the world a better place by telling kids not to say "I can't," but instead to say "I can." This will make the world better because more people will do good things.

Kerry L., *Grade 5*

2 I will try to make the world a better place by not making negative comments. If everyone stopped making negative comments, then hopefully everyone would be happier.

Melinda G., *Grade 8*

3 One way I could help make the world better is by making signs that say "smile" on them. I would put these signs all over. I think everyone would feel better from these signs.

Challis M., *Grade 8*

4 We should simply appreciate the world while it lasts.

Kiyett B., *Grade 7*

5 I would tell everyone to not be so negative with each other and to find a positive quality in someone and encourage them to let it shine.

Stacy L., *Grade 9*

6 We should wake up each morning with a positive attitude and be thankful for another day.

Stacie D., *Grade 4*

FEED THE WORLD

7 I will send all my broccoli to poor countries instead of throwing it away!

                                                    Katherine P., *Grade 6*

8 I hope to make this place better by inventing a pill that could be your breakfast, lunch, and dinner.

                                                    Emily D., *Grade 6*

9 To make this world a better place, I think it would be good for Bill Gates to buy everybody a new cow so we would never run out of milk and could make our own cheese, ice cream, yogurt, and butter. Then there would be more room in the grocery stores to have more cookie aisles and not so many refrigerator aisles that we freeze in when we go to the store.

                                                  Timothy S., *Grade 6*

10 I would grow extra food in my garden and give the food to shelters that feed the hungry. I could also convince other kids who garden to do the same thing.
          Eileen M., *Grade 4*

11 I would help the world by taking Brussels sprouts out of business. That would make a lot of kids happy.
          Kevin P., *Grade 4*

12 I will make a magic powder to make food taste better. This powder will help kids and parents eat their vegetables and other healthy foods to get stronger.
          John C., *Grade 5*

13 I would make clothes out of food. First I would make molds of clothes, and then I would put food in a blender and pour the food in the molds. This way, when you grow out of your clothes you could eat them!
          Jordan B., *Grade 6*

14 I think we can make the world a better place by sprinkling life skills over our world like salt and pepper. We would be seasoned with caring, responsibility, friendship, effort, flexibility, problem solving, common sense, and organization.
          Taylor M., *Grade 1*

15 I will invent a machine that will turn grass clippings into food for all the hungry, so there will be no starvation in the world. It will also be inexpensive, so anyone could buy it.

Breanna G., *Grade 6*

16 One thing I would do is build a huge greenhouse on an island where food could be grown for hungry people and animals. Everyone in the world would contribute seeds—even a small contribution would help.

Ellen D., *Grade 6*

17 I would open an ice-cream shop worldwide and give everyone an ice-cream cone free of charge. Then life would be sweeter for all of us.

Alexandra B., *Grade 4*

18 If I could change the world I would first change the school food. That would make a lot of kids happy.

Renee C., *Grade 7*

19 In the new millennium everything will turn into different kinds of chocolate. Cars will be made of caramel chocolate, and buildings will be made of coconut chocolate.

Daniel M., *Grade 5*

20 The world would be a better place if we had cars that used leftover food as fuel.

Lisa G., *Grade 6*

21 I would start a petition against the school food, so kids would be able to have a good and nutritious meal every day.

Ralph H., *Grade 6*

22 I would put candy all over the place—you would find candy on flowers, and gummy bears on trees!

Michelle B., *Grade 5*

23 What I'll do is encourage people to eat right and exercise, so they won't get clogged arteries from being large couch potatoes!

Desireé S., *Grade 6*

24 All the schools should have a McDonald's in them!

Velvet T., *Grade 7*

MAKE NEW FRIENDS

25 I'm going to make next year the best year by making friends with all the people who are new at our school.

Grant M., *Grade 6*

26 We could start being nicer to other people and making some friends. Then maybe that could help stop different countries from being enemies.

Hannah H., *Grade 6*

27 As an individual one can't do much to change the world, but when joined by a few friends, can move mountains!

Kelliann M., *Grade 9*

28 I would make sure everyone has a friend.

Stephanie N., *Grade 6*

29 I would make friends with kids who don't have one.

Jake S., *Grade 1*

30 I'll try to make friends with older people and new kids that move onto my block. I'll invite them over for supper and slip nice letters into their mailbox.

Haley K., *Grade 2*

31 The world would be more fun if there were more friends for everyone.

Simone D., *Kindergarten*

32 I would start by making a friend. It's the first step to peace.

Christina D., *Grade 7*

MULTI-MEDIA FOR THE MILLENNIUM

33 I could make the world a better place by trying to convince the cable TV networks and other networks to take the obscene programs off the air.

Sarah G., Grade 6

34 I want to focus on communication—not like getting better telephones, but by being more open with other countries.

Chailyn T., Grade 9

35 I would welcome the new millennium with increased communication—the old-fashioned way—with a pen pal! We could make the world smaller with an international pen pal, exchanging ideas and cultural experiences and family values.

Brianne L., Grade 7

36 I would try to get parents to watch the television ratings. They are there for a reason and should not be ignored.

Daniel G., *Grade 8*

37 I will encourage kids to watch less violent movies and shows so they wouldn't encourage kids to do things they will regret.

Colleen M., *Grade 5*

38 I feel children should petition the television stations to limit the violence and vulgarity. I think they should limit these topics because it is affecting the behavior of children.

Matthew P., *Grade 6*

39 I would like to see better television shows for children and grown-ups. Like shows about sharing, caring, and being nice to each other. This would make people better.

Jonathan G., *Grade 1*

TAKE A LOOK AT YOURSELF

40 To make the world a better place you might want to start being honest if you're not already.

Casey G., *Grade 6*

41 Many people today are too much alike. Everyone dresses the same and acts the same. We need to stop trying to fit in and be the same, and start spending time developing individual personalities.

Andrew S., *Grade 7*

42 Before I make a judgment about someone, I will try to see things from that person's point of view.

Linda N., *Grade 7*

43 We could stop stereotyping people by their appearance.

Jacquelyn R., *Grade 8*

44 I could listen more and that would make the world better because then I won't make a mistake that might cause global warfare.

Ryan G., *Grade 7*

45 I will be patient and wait until someone is done talking, and not say things like "come on" or "hurry up."

Michelle G., *Grade 4*

46 To make this world a better place: think before you act.

Janelle N., *Grade 6*

47 I'll try to influence people to be understanding, kind, giving, and accepting of others by acting the same and trying to be a respected role model.

Cherise K., *Grade 8*

48 Instead of trying to change the world, why not start by examining ourselves!

Martina M., *Grade 9*

49 I will try to always be happy and be a good boy and student.

Chad P., *Grade 1*

50 I would want everyone to learn how to forgive.

Samantha M., *Grade 6*

51 I can make the world a better place by not being so greedy. Instead of getting something every time I go to a store, I should save my money for something more important, like college or a car.

Tyler B., *Grade 6*

52 I can make myself a better person! Then when I become a better person, I can influence others around me, and they can all be honest.

Alina M., *Grade 7*

53 The world would be a better place if everyone would not take more than they give.

Brian K., *Grade 6*

54 We can stop making assumptions and blaming people for things they did not do!

Shannon B., *Grade 8*

55 I could get my act together in school, listen to my mother and father more often, and stop daydreaming in class and getting into fights.

Augustine S., *Grade 8*

56 The best way to make a better world is to develop your talents or hobbies. I will use my singing talent to bring joy and happiness to all who need it.

Karya R., *Grade 8*

THE JOY OF READING

57 I plan to make the world a better place by reading at least ten books.

Mark O., *Grade 7*

58 I think the world would be better if we invented waterproof, glow-in-the-dark books. Kids could read in bed at night without anyone knowing, and they could spill milk on their books or leave them out in the rain, and nothing would get ruined.

Asha S., *Grade 6*

59 I can read to pre-schoolers so they get a larger vocabulary and learn a lot. Plus, it's fun!

Erin H., *Grade 4*

60 I would invent a book that you can jump into, so reading can be more interesting. More kids would read these books.

Marie N., *Grade 6*

61 I could help everybody in the world by reading children's books at every orphanage. This will give all children an inspiration to read.

Doug Y., Grade 7

62 We can make the world a better place if we use less energy. We could watch less TV and read more.

Brian W., Grade 6

63 I will help the disabled and the young children learn to read. I will provide them with books, either ones I have gathered or ones I have made for them specifically. Together we will share the reading adventure, and they also will learn to love the world of words.

Malynda B., Grade 5

64 I would buy everyone a set of chapter books by winning the Lottery 50 or 100 times, so everyone would be able to read and enjoy them for free.

Brent W., Grade 5

WE THE PEOPLE

65 In order to make this world a better place, a woman must run for president.

Jennifer G., Grade 7

66 I think they should let kids vote. The president is our president, too, and I think we should be able to take part in the election.

Stephanie R., Grade 6

67 I can encourage my parents to vote for each branch of government, because the better our government, the better the world will be overall. People need to stop complaining and start voting!

Mujeeb H., Grade 6

68 The thing we could do to make the world a better place is to lower the age to become president to 30. There are young minds with great ideas, and I want these people to have a chance.

Bryan T., Grade 7

69 I would like to be the first female president and also the youngest president. I will make a shopping center in the basement of the White House so all the poor people can get free clothes.

Meghan D., Grade 7

70 If I had a chance to make the world better, I would drop taxes. I think it would be better if there were no taxes at all.

Terra R., Grade 6

71 To make the world better, I think girls should run the world. If girls ran the world there wouldn't be any wars, because boys use war to settle their differences. Girls would just say, "Come on girlfriend, let's talk it over at lunch."

Shelley P., Grade 6

72 I can help make the world a better place by being the first kid president. Then I could help children get a better education.

Laura B., Grade 6

WORLD PEACE AND INTERNATIONAL RELATIONS

73 I will send a letter to every country requesting their help with a flag of unity. The flag will consist of each country's symbol of peace, joined on one flag for all to remember why we are here on this planet.

Hollie L., *Grade 7*

74 I will be the first woman to go to Mars to make peace with the Martian dudes, in order to create universal peace.

Krista A., *Grade 6*

75 If making speeches to fight against violence can make a change, I will do everything in my power to reach the heart of the people.

Kemesha C., *Grade 9*

76 We can make this world a better place by making more laws against racism.

Deena A., *Grade 8*

77 I will write a letter to the President suggesting that instead of having a real war we have a really big paintball war. That way nobody gets hurt, injured, or killed.

Jason D., *Grade 6*

78 I would make all the countries form one big country so we could be all together in peace.

Diana C., *Grade 8*

79 I will change the world by designing a system of currency that the whole world will use. It will make it easier on everyone, once everybody gets used to the new system.

Greg W., *Grade 8*

80 My goal is to make 366 new friends around the world by sending a letter to one pen pal a day. I hope that the kids who receive my letters will be inspired to continue this idea and make their own international friends.

James M., *Grade 5*

81 I would universalize weights, measures, and language to drastically improve trade and communication between countries.

Paul M., *Grade 7*

82. To make the world a better place I will start humming a catchy song. People will hear me hum and hopefully will start humming the tune also. Finally, as more people start humming, the world will stand united under a hum.

Mark M., *Grade 8*

YOUNG AND OLD ALIKE

83 I would put pets in all nursing homes to make the world a better place, because pets help elderly people so they live longer and stay healthier.

Kelly A., *Grade 7*

84 I could become a mentor to a younger child who has a bad home environment or has been hurt in any way. If everyone was a mentor to just one person, it would make a difference in the world.

Gentry J., *Grade 7*

85 I plan to go to hospitals and visit all the sick children to cheer them up.

Stephanie F., *Grade 7*

86 I will get clowns to visit poor, sick, and lonely children.

Abbe L., *Grade 7*

87 I could teach more seniors how to use computers.

Randy B., *Grade 6*

88 I could do volunteer work such as going to a nursing home and just talking with people to make them feel better.

Deepa P., *Grade 7*

89 I can help the world by helping older people, by buying and delivering their groceries for them.

Anna Z., *Grade 8*

90 I can ask kids to play and do things. This way if kids are busy doing things they can't do bad things like smoke.

Christian F., *Grade 6*

91 I could teach young children how to swim safely. If everyone would learn how to swim there would be fewer drownings.

Amanda O., *Grade 6*

92 I could help my friends with their homework, which will help them and the teachers.

Sara W., *Grade 7*

93 I can help my mother start a day-care center for both children and the elderly. The elderly people could help with the children, and the children would have a special friend to read to them and help them.

Andi L., *Grade 7*

94 I could form a homework club that would benefit kids who did not have time to do their homework at home. This would improve the grades of many students, and thus improve the passing rate.

Michael Z., *Grade 8*

95 I can try to entice more kids to play guitar, because I think it could help kids stay away from crime if they played guitar.

Jordan B., *Grade 7*

96 I could clean up houses for old people so they don't hurt themselves.

Stacey P., *Grade 6*

97 Children without families can be adopted by people who love them. I will ask my parents to adopt someone who is alone.

Lindsay J., *Grade 2*

98 I would attempt to get kids off the street by organizing team sports and recreation parks, starting in my own neighborhood.

Wesley B., *Grade 9*

99 I could help kids do things they don't know how to do, like ride a bike and play chess.

Philippe D., *Grade 7*

OUR FURRY FRIENDS

100 To make the world a better place we should allow cats to rule the world. Then everyone would sleep 18 hours a day, keep clean, and eat plenty of food. Everyone will have lots of toys, a nice, warm fireplace, and of course, someone to love.

Lydia G., Grade 8

101 I would build a giant animal shelter where animals roam free without cages.

Justin P., Grade 6

102 I would get blood samples of all endangered animals and clone them.

Kevin L., Grade 6

103 I can make the world a better place by adopting a homeless animal.

Jennes N., Grade 2

104 Something I can do to make the world a better place is go to the animal shelters or pounds and volunteer to help wash, groom, and walk the dogs to keep them healthy.

Analisa E., *Grade 7*

105 I could make the world a better place by taking stray dogs off the street and training them to be Seeing Eye dogs, rescue dogs, or police dogs. They would have a home and be able to help people and maybe save lives.

Dianna B., *Grade 7*

106 I hope that in the next millennium kids can help calm the homeless animals in shelters by taking them for walks and playing classical music for them.

Kenzie B., *Grade 3*

107 I could open up a pet shop and once a month open it earlier than usual and keep it open later to give away free pets all day long.

Sarah S., *Grade 5*

108 We should cut all the rings on plastic six-packs to help save the animals.

Lacy D., *Grade 6*

109 There should be bigger and better zoos, and they would have more plants. Animals would feel free and wouldn't be disturbed.

Emilee N., *Grade 5*

110 I am going to save animals, especially endangered animals, by going to them and feeding them, taking care of them and loving them.

Nicole A., *Grade 1*

111 I am going to get a kitty and a puppy for everybody in the world.

Kevin M., *Grade 6*

112 I would take in all the stray cats and dogs so they would have a safe place to live.

Traci H., *Grade 7*

113 I can make a better world by being nice to animals. By having my pets fixed I will reduce the numbers of unwanted animals. I will also make sure my pets have the best medical attention.

Lanessa P., *Grade 5*

114 I will volunteer to work with abandoned animals at animal shelters.

Hope G., *Grade 8*

115 I will help the world by helping 2,000 wild horses, especially wild mustangs, from being captured by people who want to keep them and tame them.

Stacia S., *Grade 6*

116 I could make a dog wash that would be similar to a car wash. Dogs would wear goggles, ear plugs, and be hooked to a leash. Then they would sit in a wagon and go through the soap washer, rinse, and be towel-dried.

Kendra L., *Grade 8*

117 We could save a lot of animals from oil spills if the oil companies started to transport oil by air instead of by sea.

Christina L., *Grade 7*

COMMUNITY HELPERS

118 To see youth volunteering in the community is a very rare sight, but if they start, it would make this world a better place to live in.

Precious R., *Grade 9*

119 I can make the new millennium great by volunteering for sports, church, and school groups in my community to make it a better place to live and play.

Katie G., *Grade 6*

120 Everyone should use that treasured feeling you get from helping out, turn off the television for just a half hour or so, and do something in the neighborhood—small or large, it all helps. All it takes to make a difference is a gesture, and if everyone makes the smallest gesture then all the corners of the world would be changed for the best.

Aria S., *Grade 9*

121 We could take the abandoned buildings and remodel them so they can be used for the community.

Gerard P., *Grade 7*

CRIME-FIGHTERS

122 I can make the world a better place by forming a team of volunteers to help out our town's police department by working on smaller crimes such as stolen bicycles. This would give the police more time to work on larger crimes.

Wes T., Grade 8

123 I would make all the criminals who are behind bars spend their time cleaning up their cities and states.

Alexandria S., Grade 3

124 I would take all the guns, knives, and dangerous things from all the people in the world and recycle them into useful materials.

Sharnese G., Grade 7

125 I would take all the guns in the world and replace them with water guns.
Amy M., *Grade 6*

126 I could help make the world a better place by starting a neighborhood crime watch.
Kristi T., *Grade 7*

127 I will make a remote control that turns cars off during high-speed chases. The cops will be able to punch a code, and the remote will turn the car off.
Cody S., *Grade 7*

128 We can make robocops in every town. They would stop crime and violence, and play games with little kids if they want to.
Joseph Q., *Grade 6*

129 I could make the world better by inventing a gun-detecting machine that will detect guns in a city and tell the police where they are. This will allow police to track down criminals with guns.
Peter W., *Grade 5*

130 I would hire aliens to stand guard at all stores. If someone tries to steal something, the aliens would blast them with a disintegrating ray. People could also use them at their houses for $250.99.
Stephen C., *Grade 6*

131 I want to make the world a better place by having a rocket sent to outer space with everybody in prison inside it. I will leave it there for a LONG time—I really doubt there will be any more problems with prisoners after they come back.

Jason S., *Grade 6*

132 I will make the world better by destroying street weapons.

Francisco B., *Grade 8*

ALIEN ADVENTURES

133 I will fly to Mars and find out how the living conditions are there, then make another Earth, only without guns and drugs.

Gina P., *Grade 8*

134 I could invent a space station that could house an entire country. All the food would be fresh-made, and the air pure. The space station would have every modern advancement—it would be fabulous.

John P., *Grade 7*

135 People should send messages to space saying, "Aliens can land on our friendly Earth." We should also make a huge airport so aliens can land here.

Itzett R., *Grade 6*

136 The world would be a better place if everyone were an alien! Everybody would look cool, and they would be intelligent.

Brook P., *Grade 7*

137 I will go into space and make the world turn slower, so the days will be longer for more sleep time, play time, school time, and best of all, longer weekends!

Ashley D., *Grade 5*

138 We will be able to go to other planets, which would each be assigned different categories. For example, Mars would be for all the robbers, so Earth could be for all the good people in the world.

Michele F., *Grade 5*

139 I would make this world a better place by having an interplanetary mart where humans and aliens could trade goods with each other.

Chris K., *Grade 5*

140 I can turn into a muscle man, build a big net out of cloth, and put every person and animal in the net. Then I would bring them to Mars and start the world over.

Daryl H., *Grade 6*

141 We should go to another planet. Boys would have to go to Jupiter, girls would go to Mars, and parents would live on Mercury.

Angela P., *Grade 6*

142 I think we should dispose of all the other planets and galaxies so no bat-nosed, tentacle-waving, lava-drinking, three-eyed aliens can take over Earth!

John C., *Grade 6*

MAKING THE GRADE

143 I think that all school students should have to wear school uniforms. This way there would be less discrimination among social groups, but students could still express their individuality through their hair, makeup, and shoes.

Katrina M., *Grade 7*

144 I'll make three-day weekends for school so kids will only have to go to school four days a week and be happier.

Alexandria A., *Grade 4*

145 I think we should have Mondays off from school.

Jenny C., *Grade 7*

146 One idea for making the world a better place is to have smaller classes to help prevent arguments and fights, and to help students comprehend their work better.

Marvin D., Grade 7

147 If I could make the world a better place I would outlaw chalkboards, because sometimes when I write on them it makes a screeching noise that makes my skin crawl.

Jayson V., Grade 4

148 Since students are always getting to class late, remote-controlled lockers would be a big help, because sometimes the lock combination won't work or you can't find your key.

Tara N., Grade 7

149 I would have the schools buy new supplies every year so the new kids won't have to use broken crayons and worn-out markers, and they won't get books with ripped and written-on pages.

Kaycee I., Grade 5

150 I will ask the principal to let kids have physical education every day so kids get more exercise.

Bennett R., Grade 6

151 I want to improve schools by letting children design and help build their own playground equipment. This would reinforce working cooperatively, and develop pride and sense of ownership in their own school.

Catherine M., *Grade 5*

152 We can make the world better by taking the dogs and cats from animal shelters and bringing them to the schools. The children will be able to take care of the pets, and the pets will be happy with their new homes.

Tim F., *Grade 5*

153 To make this world a better place we need to come to school in limos.

Lynette T., *Grade 7*

154 We should keep the schools clean and make more rules to make sure kids clean up their school property.

Angela P., *Grade 5*

155 I'm going to start a system that does your homework for you.

Gina C., *Grade 6*

156 I could bring up the suggestion that everyone's first class in school be sign language, so everyone could communicate in peace.

Lauren Y., *Grade 7*

157 I would ask the president if schools can have a field trip every month, two computers in each room, and tables instead of desks.

Jonathan G., *Grade 7*

158 I would get new textbooks for all schools so kids in the new millennium don't have to learn the same thing over and over again.

Melissa K., *Grade 6*

159 In the new millennium I will be in school preparing for my future as a businessman or business owner. I will get a job after school so I can prove to everybody that I am a good worker.

Matthew P., *Grade 8*

160 The way to make the world a better place is to have more fundraisers in schools so the schools would have more money for field trips and equipment.

Jonathan G., *Grade 5*

161 I would encourage kids in my school to remember the janitors and bus drivers by making them cards or saying nice words to them. These people help us a lot during the school year!

Tristan S., *Grade 4*

162 I will start a campaign that will teach teens to stay in school.

Jennifer R., *Grade 7*

163 I would pass a law ensuring all students have laptop computers. This would be to the teachers' advantage so they could read our writing.

Glenn C., *Grade 8*

164 I would make teachers teach exciting subjects such as fencing, boxing, and wrestling instead of boring subjects.

Daniel C., *Grade 8*

165 What I would do is persuade the government to give more moral education in schools so people will be more aware of their actions.

Mariola R., *Grade 8*

166 I would start a fitness club at school to keep everyone within their specified weight group. This would make people feel a lot better about themselves.

Sean S., *Grade 8*

167 What would make the world better would be to have school every other day. When you were home from school you could do schoolwork from a computer.

Jireh H., *Grade 6*

168 I would like to have bathrooms in every classroom, and a little lunch stand in our class.
Tim M., *Grade 6*

169 Better schools with many rooms would make the world a better place. Schools with no bullies, schools with all good teachers, a school with eight floors.
George F., *Grade 1*

170 I will be kind to substitute teachers.
Marissa P., *Grade 7*

171 Because students really don't want to come to school, I would assist computer specialists to create an advanced, home-based teaching program on CD-ROM, allowing students to become better educated in a home environment.
Alexander C., *Grade 9*

172 I would improve the world by having kids go to school in their pajamas if they wanted to. This way kids would not have to worry about what to wear in the morning, there would be less kids late to school every day, and the kids would be more comfortable during the day.
Laura E., *Grade 4*

173 I can invent a computer that contains all school subjects for home-schooled children. It will have a program like a regular school day, with reading and math class, recess breaks, and lunch.

Brian L., *Grade 6*

174 We should spend more time outside. Therefore, we should have a school building with moveable walls and roof. Then we could choose to be inside or outside.

Claire H., *Grade 5*

EVERY DAY'S A HOLIDAY

175 I will start a new holiday called "Unlearn Prejudice Day." On this day, all people, black and white, Jewish and Christian, rich and poor, will get together. People who are different will become partners and choose five fun activities to do together and forget about how they are different.

Scott C., *Grade 4*

176 We should make a holiday called "Spend None Day." No one could spend money on that day, and all the money saved would go to the needy.

Andrea P., *Grade 6*

177 We should wish everyone a "happy birthday" every day so when their real birthday comes, they wouldn't complain about being a whole year older.

Holly O., *Grade 6*

178 We should have a "Hello Day," where everyone gets the day off and we all have to say "hello" to people. We could send a prize patrol out to give prizes to a perfect "hello" person in every state.

Sarah Z., *Grade 6*

179 I would start a free service to help all the disabled people. I would do jobs they needed help with, like yard work, cleaning, or just visiting with them.

Robert G., *Grade 7*

180 I can make the world a better place by making toys for poor children.

Devannie R., *Grade 2*

181 I will go to homes for the blind to read and talk with people and make them smile.

Brianna T., *Grade 8*

182 I would get people to sign petitions to build parks in each state for kids who have disabilities. The mayor will build two or three of these parks, and after that, people in other states and countries will do the same thing. This way all the kids who have disabilities can play, too!

Charris A., *Grade 4*

FAMILY TIES

183 In the Year 2000 I plan to do all the 2,000 tasks my mom tells me to do every day.

Laura B., *Grade 8*

184 To make the world better, stay close with your family and never let anyone, even your best friend, talk you into trying drugs or acting violently.

Chad C., *Grade 6*

185 I can make the world better by helping my brother with his homework.

Leonard D., *Grade 2*

186 I would write a book telling parents how important they are to us, how we need their support during our growth, and for them to listen to what we need to say.

Maria O., *Grade 8*

187 I can be more kind and patient with my brothers and my sister. I could also help clean the house or help my mom with some laundry.

Renee H., *Grade 7*

188 I can make the world a better place by trying to keep peace with my family, and being more patient with my parents. I could try to be a better person and be a good example to others.

Erin T., *Grade 7*

189 I can help my dad stop smoking, and go to the grocery store for my family because they are always busy.

Casey S., *Grade 3*

190 To make the world a better place I will share and be good. I will be nice to my mom and dad.

Sally W., *Grade 2*

191 I can stop fighting with my brother and sister. Others will see this and also get along.

Amie D., *Grade 5*

192 We should wake up when Mommy tells us to!

Alexis C., *Kindergarten*

193 I will make the world better by helping my mom around the house with the baby. This might influence other children to help also.

David G., *Grade 5*

EARTH-FRIENDLY IDEAS

194 I would try to stop the factories from dumping all the chemicals in the water, because it kills the fish and other animals, which might include us.

Annie P., *Grade 7*

195 One of the ways we could make the world better is on every second Thursday of the month, every citizen of the world should pick up 2 pieces of trash each.

Ross A., *Grade 5*

196 I think one thing I can do is not litter. All the pants I wear have pockets, so why not just stuff the trash in my pockets?

Pete C., *Grade 7*

197 I will start recycling my homework papers so we will have less garbage.

Ricky S., *Grade 3*

198 I think we should have at least four Earth Days a year so the world will be clean as gold.

Robby S., *Grade 2*

199 I would put a recycling bin on every road in the world so no one would throw garbage on the street anymore.

Kayla D., *Grade 6*

200 I will write a letter to the president asking him to issue a law that if you cut down a tree you have to plant another tree.

Alicia T., *Grade 7*

201 I think schools should start cleaning programs in the spring by finding a park and spending a day cleaning it.

Elena R., *Grade 7*

202 I would make a floating, ocean-cleaning robot that would be powered by waves. It would clean up oil spills and trash, and help the animals hurt by the oil spills.

Conor W., *Grade 5*

203 I will try to invent a machine that will work like a water filter—people will put it on top of their houses, and it will purify polluted air.

Jenna B., *Grade 7*

204 I would launch nuclear weapons filled with garbage to the sun, so it would melt away to nothingness.

Corey S., Grade 7

205 We can write to companies that destroy rain forests for products and tell them that we will boycott them unless they start to appreciate the rain forests.

Abigail C., Grade 8

206 At the parks, we should take only pictures and leave only footprints.

Rob M., Grade 4

207 I would plant more flowers since my mom and I love to make gardens.

Amy B., Grade 6

208 If everyone does the simple things, like using two sides of the paper to save trees, we eventually can make a difference.

Nikki A., Grade 8

209 To make the world a better place, I will pick up 2,000 pieces of trash each month. I will also encourage my friends to pick up more trash, too, so the world will be cleaner.

Danielle D., Grade 7

210 I could stop using hairspray.

Jessica D., *Grade 6*

211 I would plant seeds all over the world.

Sara H., *Grade 3*

212 I could stop taking long showers and not let the water run.

Jarred P., *Grade 6*

213 We should get rid of all the aerosol cans.

Jimmy R., *Grade 6*

214 I would make the world a better place by inventing a machine that takes one mineral from a mine and multiplies it thousands of times so we have an endless source of natural resources.

R.J. N., *Grade 5*

215 I could plant trees and flowers in front of store windows, and plant trees in front of restaurants in the city.

Jennifer A., *Grade 6*

216 I would create a new wrapper for candy that would be made out of edible material for birds. After eating the candy, the wrapper could be torn into small pieces and scattered for the birds to eat.

Sheri R., *Grade 5*

217 We could raise money to help the rain forests by standing at any store with a good bucket and a sign saying "Collecting for the Rain Forests." Some kind, good citizens will donate.

Jennifer M., *Grade 6*

FOR A GOOD CAUSE

218 I could sponsor a starving child in a poor country.

Jessi B., *Grade 6*

219 I think we should educate the homeless and get people off the streets.

Dustin C., *Grade 6*

220 I could start a program in my community for citizens to donate the first 2,000 pennies they receive in change to help people who are needy.

Tracy D., *Grade 7*

221 I could save a dollar each week, and then at the end of the year donate all the money to a charity.

Joshua B., *Grade 8*

222 I would make one billion peanut butter and jelly sandwiches for the homeless and hungry.

Samantha Y., Grade 6

223 I would rebuild abandoned buildings to make homes for the homeless.

Thomas H., Grade 7

224 I can write a letter to Major League Baseball asking the president to ask the players to play for a week or at least a day without pay. Then they could give the money to the needy.

Stan G., Grade 6

225 I would ask the principal if we could have a box at school to donate clothes we don't want for poor people.

Codie R., Grade 6

226 I will help by giving lots of money to special charities, traveling to poor countries, and giving the people money.

Chris R., Grade 7

227 I will plant a garden to grow food for poor people. My garden will have lots of vegetables, especially broccoli—my favorite! My mom will help me pick the vegetables and drive me to people who are hungry.

Nicki W., Grade 2

228 We should do something about the homeless. I suggest each secure family or individual be partners with a homeless person. They will provide food and shelter, and send money once a month for three meals a day.

Alex P., *Grade 5*

229 I will collect clothes and shoes to pass out to the homeless who need to keep warm at night, or protect their toes from painful frostbite!

Anne R., *Grade 7*

230 I will work with my aunt and her friends with Habitat for Humanity to help paint and build houses for people who can't afford to have professionals do it for them.

Robert S., *Grade 6*

231 I could collect toys from my neighborhood. Then I'll take my neighbor's station wagon and drive across the nation so all the homeless kids will get new toys.

Marisa E., *Grade 6*

232 I would take away all the money in the world. People would receive any supplies they need, and there would be no rich or poor.

Sam M., *Grade 7*

HOME SWEET HOME

233 I would invent a huge airtight structure so people can live underwater. It would have an elevator that would transport people up and down.
> Scott C., *Grade 6*

234 I would make sure every house in the world had a smoke detector.
> Rachel F., *Grade 6*

235 I would make pocket-sized houses so people wouldn't have to worry about their house being robbed while they were at work, and they could take it on vacation so they wouldn't have to pay hotel fees.
> Kristen M., *Grade 6*

236 I would make houses with the same size bedrooms so kids won't fight over which room they get.
> Ryan M., *Grade 6*

237 I would want to fire-proof buildings so people would be safe, and houses wouldn't burn down and have to be rebuilt.

Andrew L., *Grade 1*

238 I would revolutionize people's lifestyles to better the world. Instead of houses above ground, the general population would live in cylindrical underground houses that would have domed plastic roofs and entrances. This would decrease storm damage and lower utility costs.

Matt K., *Grade 6*

239 The world would be a better place if houses could fly! Then you could move to different places without paying moving expenses, or packing bags and priceless possessions.

Brandon P., *Grade 4*

240 I could make the world better by making a house or garage weather-repellent. My formula would stop hurricanes, tornadoes, and other bad storms from ruining buildings.

Jenna W., *Grade 6*

241 I would change every kid's room into a mini-arcade. There would be a built-in trampoline in your bed, and ping-pong machines and a basketball hoop in the closet.

Savannah M., *Grade 6*

242 We should have a city in the sky, above the clouds, for when a tornado, hurricane, volcano, or something else bad strikes. Each person would have a transporter in their house to take them there.

Max S., *Grade 4*

243 I would put windmills at every house that people would use for natural energy. Then people wouldn't have to pay for electricity.

Brendon T., *Grade 3*

244 We can buy air tanks and live in the ocean. Then we can be like fish and swim with the dolphins and whales. We can even go see the *Titanic*.

Ashley C., *Grade 6*

GREAT INVENTIONS

245 I would invent a shot that has a sunscreen formula that lasts for five years to keep people from getting sunburned or skin cancer. It would cost $5.00.

Sami E., *Grade 6*

246 I could make a car with sweepers on the side so when I drive, the sweepers would go on the ground and sweep up the road around them. It could also have polishers on it so they could polish the roads and trees.

Hannah P., *Grade 7*

247 I would invent water fountains that were soda fountains instead.

Patricia B., *Grade 5*

248 I would mold clear plastic into shirts and jeans that you would put over your clothes so nothing can stain them. This would help the water supply.

Valerie J., *Grade 6*

249 I will make an invention to feed our dogs so it will make life easier and we won't get our hands messy.

Joseph M., *Grade 4*

250 I will invent a telepod that will transport people from once place to another in five seconds!

Josiah L., *Grade 6*

251 I will invent a talking clock that will tell me when to get dressed, brush my teeth, catch the bus, etc.

Bernard K., *Grade 5*

252 I could invent a robot that does all things mankind can do and more, like all the household chores.

Jon S., *Grade 8*

253 I will make an invention to stop drunk driving. It will sort of be like a breathalizer test that you put in your car. If you're over the level, your car won't start.

Joe A., *Grade 5*

254 I would put jets in shoes so we would be able to fly down the street.

Gavin L., *Grade 6*

255 The way I would make the world a better place is to make licorice pencils, so we can save the trees.
Nicole H., *Grade 6*

256 I can make the world better by inventing flying space shoes for people who can't walk and are in wheelchairs. They will help people feel like they really can walk and will make them happy.
Ramon C., *Grade 5*

257 I could invent a machine that prepares breakfast for people in the morning.
LaQuanda T., *Grade 5*

258 I would invent a satellite that shoots a laser at trash and then turns it into tree seeds. Then a mechanical bird would fly from the satellite, pick up the seeds, and plant them in a place that needs more trees to replace the ones that were cut down.
David S., *Grade 4*

259 I will invent a type of hairspray that is made with starch instead of harmful fluorocarbons.
Celeste S., *Grade 6*

260 I could invent a super-fast luggage carrier that runs underground to carry your homework home. This way we could ride the school bus empty-handed.
April M., *Grade 7*

261 I would invent a vacuum that would suck up all the air pollution. Then when you put it in reverse, it would shoot out clouds to fill in any holes in the ozone layer.

Ashley R., *Grade 5*

262 I would help by inventing a machine to stop air pollution toxins to help us breathe better.

Ryan F., *Grade 6*

263 I will invent a car that will run on garbage. It would keep the pollution rate down by 99% to help our ozone layer, it will help cut down on unsightly landfills, and it will help poor people afford transportation. I will also receive a prize for this invention.

Brittany S., *Grade 7*

264 I plan to make a toilet with a potpourri sprayer—there will be a button on the right side, and when you press it, potpourri would spray inside the toilet.

Amy F., *Grade 6*

265 I will make a machine that will clean any room. It will sweep, vacuum, mop, wash your clothes, and much more. You could operate it by remote control or set it on autopilot.

Charlie J., *Grade 6*

266 I will invent a car that runs on water instead of gas. That way it wouldn't hurt anything, and it would be a lot cheaper!

Ashley B., *Grade 6*

267 I could make a microwave oven that can cook anything in just one second—anything from a big turkey to hot chocolate.

Haley B., *Grade 8*

268 I would design a pair of sneakers that change into shoes for people who are in a rush and don't have time to change shoes.

Melissa G., *Grade 7*

269 I would help this world by helping to make a labor-saving device. It would be a chair attached to a refrigerator, which would help lazy people like myself, so we would not have to get up for a snack during a sports event or show.

Ian K., *Grade 5*

270 I would invent a machine that would make animals immune to gunshots, so it would be harder for poachers to kill them.

Rachael B., *Grade 7*

271 There are many tornadoes in the world, but the warning we have today is still not good enough. I would like to invent a tool that can go inside the tornado to see how it works so the warnings will be better.

Christy S., *Grade 6*

272 I would invent a car that uses grass for fuel instead of gas. It won't pollute the air, and all you have to do is take grass from your yard.

Breah G., *Grade 7*

273 I could make a chip that goes into every person's head at the age of 11 that would have all the fundamentals of learning (literature, math, science), so school would not be necessary, and everyone would be educated equally.

Elizabeth W., *Grade 9*

274 I think we should make electric gloves and socks for when it's cold, and air-conditioned underwear for when it's hot.

Sammy J., *Grade 6*

275 I will prepare to be a scientist by trying to make a smoke-free ashtray that will get rid of the smoke.

Ramon C., *Grade 8*

276 I would invent something that would let doctors experience your pain so that they could tell if you were sick enough to miss school.

Dakota W., *Grade 6*

277 I think we should have shoes that will keep us from falling down. When we start to fall, the shoes will bring us back up before we hit the ground.

Kay F., *Grade 5*

278 We should invent a pill that people can take so they don't have to wear glasses.

Sarah S., *Grade 5*

279 I would make a button that goes on your wrist that would let you be anyone you want to be in the world.

David B., *Grade 5*

280 I will invent a splash-on paint wallpaper. All you would have to do is throw the paint on the wall and it would come out looking like a wallpaper design.

Chrissy P., *Grade 5*

281 I can invent a machine that turns dirt into food for the poor people of the world.

Molly R., *Grade 5*

282 I want to make edible dishes so no one ever has to do the dishes again. They will also save energy because nobody will have to run a dishwasher.

Sabrina B., *Grade 7*

283 I will invent a machine that makes schools safer. This machine will make swings, slides, monkey bars, and everything safer so that kids won't get hurt.

Tim C., *Grade 5*

284 I would find a way to make all electric items solar-powered. Then people would have low electricity bills, and they wouldn't have to buy batteries either.

Shannon W., *Grade 5*

285 I could invent a robot to do students' homework. Just push three buttons: on, subject, and operation. This will encourage kids to like homework.

Angela C., *Grade 5*

286 I would invent a free device that would help control air pollution. It would be on every heating system, car, moped, dirt bike, and other off-road vehicle.

Jackie K., *Grade 6*

287 I would create a machine that would give you anything you want. All you have to do is spell it out on the alphabet buttons.

                                                Charlotte S., *Grade 6*

288 I will make a money tree so everyone would have money. When you pull money off the tree, more money would grow.

                                                Jimmy R., *Grade 2*

289 I think we should invent robot soldiers who can fight all our battles for us, so people won't get killed.

                                                Cody K., *Grade 7*

PLAY BY PLAY

290 To make this world a better place I would let women play in the NFL, because when I watch football it makes me want to do that when I grow up. This would make it fairer for women.

Sophia M., *Grade 6*

291 I would put football in the Olympics.

Ryan W., *Grade 6*

292 I would try to make the world a better place by bringing Michael Jordan out of retirement.

Eric S., *Grade 8*

293 I would build a free stadium to inspire people to play basketball. I would invite famous basketball players to sign autographs.

Nick D., *Grade 5*

294 I would give everybody a dirt bike and helmet so everybody would be happy, because dirt bikes give you a special feeling that you'll never get riding a bike.

Chris M., *Grade 7*

295 One way I could make the world a better place is to have good sportsmanship, like not being mad when I lose.

Samantha S., *Grade 8*

296 I would invent more sports that everyone would be able to play, including disabled people. I think more sports would make more people happy.

Brendon G., *Grade 7*

297 I will try to get my city to put up more basketball hoops, so everyone can stay in shape.

Jon S., *Grade 8*

298 I will invent a new sport that everyone can play, no matter how old they are, so people can play outside instead of sitting inside. This sport will be in the Olympics someday, because it shows unity between different ages.

Cari S., *Grade 6*

MAKE ME LAUGH!

299 I would carry an odorizer in my backpack, not for *my* smell but for school bus smells. I have been a witness to many smells on the bus ride, so this would be not only for me, but for people in neighboring seats.

Tim H., *Grade 7*

300 I would tell everyone to laugh for two reasons: it livens you up, and you burn calories. So laugh!

Peggy W., *Grade 8*

301 We should eat cookies and hot fudge for lunch, and ride a roller coaster every Sunday!

Sarah G., *Grade 3*

302 I will start putting away the toaster. This will decrease the number of times my mom has to yell at me, which will decrease the amount of hot air let into the atmosphere. This might help slow global warming.

Caitlin F., *Grade 7*

303 I can make the world a better place by running comedy clubs all around the country, because humor can help people fight cancer and other diseases.

Jeramy S., *Grade 5*

304 I would invent a Y2K spider that would catch the Y2K bug and eat it. Then the spider would fix all the damage the Y2K bug caused!

Andrew C., *Grade 4*

305 I would shave all the black cats' hair off, then nobody would have bad luck!

Cimmeron T., *Grade 5*

TO OUR HEALTH

306 I will do well in school so I can become a scientist. Then I hope to find a cure for illnesses that make people suffer.

Amanda E., *Grade 5*

307 I would make a machine that could cure a disease just by seeing it, no matter what. If I can't do that, I will find many cures when I become a doctor!

Jeanine M., *Grade 7*

308 I would give money to scientists to help them discover cures for mental retardation and depression. I think a lot of people would have better lives if there were cures for these things.

Scott J., *Grade 6*

309 We should open hospitals that have free or low prices for smaller wounds (stitches, x-rays, etc.) for all sorts of people instead of hospitals that cost lots of money for minor fix-ups.

Matthew G., *Grade 6*

310 I would find a way to make needles painless for all kids that have to get shots.

MacKenzie F., *Grade 6*

311 I would invent a healthy cigarette that would contain vitamins. This would help cut down on cancer and supply needed vitamins to people.

Joseph F., *Grade 8*

312 I could invent a medicine that tastes like soda pop so kids would like it. It could cure things like the common cold.

Karley K., *Grade 5*

313 I will make a shrinking ray so people can go into other people who are sick and find the cause of it.

Chad S., *Grade 5*

314 Something I could do is to talk people into wearing sunscreen so there would be a lot less skin cancer around the world.

Theresa F., *Grade 7*

315 I will help promote a program for children who do not have health insurance. The program will provide for all necessary prescriptions and treatments for disabilities as wells as illnesses. Our children deserve this.

Kimberly S., *Grade 8*

316 We should give more money to medical researchers.

Jason A., *Grade 6*

317 I would find a cure for the common cold.

Emily W., *Grade 5*

318 I would like to invent a machine that would implant anti-cells in your body that would completely wipe out germs and diseases.

Alex D., *Grade 5*

SAY NO TO SUBSTANCE ABUSE

319 I will make life better by pledging to be drug-free.

Carlos Z., *Grade 5*

320 I would like to help change our world by banning all tobacco products such as chewing tobacco, pipe tobacco, cigars, and cigarettes.

Kimberly C., *Grade 7*

321 I would start a drug-free after-school club. If you say "no" to drugs you can join this club, and we can play games and hang out together.

Michael R., *Grade 5*

322 We should make more places smoke-free.

Lucas F., *Grade 6*

323 People should be required to get a Breathalyzer test when they are ready to leave a bar. If they fail the test, they must have a designated driver so there will be fewer accidents.

David H., *Grade 5*

324 I can make the world a better place by not buying drugs from gangsters, to put them out of business so they can't make money to buy bullets and guns to kill people.

Sean K., *Grade 5*

325 I would write a letter to our city officials asking them to pass a law that would ban smoking in public places.

Bobby D., *Grade 7*

GETTING AROUND

326 I think the biggest improvement we could get is vehicles that run on tracks. If cars ran on electric tracks there would be less wrecks because people couldn't hit each other head-on. It would also take less time to get where you're going.

Amos B., Grade 7

327 I would like to create interdimensional travel that would help us find new worlds to support life.

Brian M., Grade 8

328 Everyone should have a set of wings, so some of the traffic and pollution problems could be solved. Plus, it would be like angels everywhere on earth.

Brittany B., Grade 6

329 I would make cars like bumper cars so there would be fewer accidents. Kids could also drive them and would have lots of fun.

Eugene S., *Grade 5*

330 Kids should have their own cars and our own lanes with padded walls so no one can get hurt. You would have to be just eight years old to drive.

Laura B., *Grade 5*

331 I'm going to make life better and easier by telling companies to make a new car called a compucar. All you have to do is type in where you want to go and it will take you there.

Robert S., *Grade 4*

332 I would make flying bikes so you wouldn't have to worry about airplanes in the sky.

Cortney B., *Grade 6*

333 We could ride elephants. That would stop pollution and those annoying car horns. I haven't figured out how to rig the seat belts yet, but it would be like everyone having a convertible.

Eli A., *Grade 6*

334 I would invent a kids' airline that would serve good food like pizza, tacos, and macaroni and cheese. This airline would go anywhere in the world. There would only be two adults on board: the pilot and co-pilot.

Maxine K., *Grade 5*

335 I would make walking and biking trails to cut down on the pollution caused by cars.

David P., *Grade 7*

336 I would propose a law for all businesses to start car pools to cut down on air pollution and congestion on the highways around the world.

Matthew D., *Grade 8*

337 The world would be better if we had flying cars.

Yomaira G., *Grade 7*

338 I will stay off the roads when I get my permit because I know I will most likely get into many accidents!

Jennifer S., *Grade 7*

339 I could build a bridge across the Atlantic Ocean that would save money on airline tickets. This bridge would have restaurants, shops, and gas stations.

Joseph M., *Grade 7*

340 We could have super markets on wheels so people without cars could walk outside and shop.

T.J. D., *Grade 6*

341 I would make the world a better place by giving everybody a car.

Yuri C., *Grade 7*

342 I am going to make a car-pool matching service so people can find out if anyone who lives by them is going to the same place.

Amanda D., *Grade 6*

343 I would campaign to eliminate aggravating and dangerous roadways, like one-way tunnels, six-way intersections, and roads that are cracked and crumbled. This would decrease accidents, hence Earth would be a safer place.

Daniel F., *Grade 7*

344 What would make the world better is to have more sidewalks for people, so people will not have a reason to walk on the street except to cross it.

Uchenna L., *Grade 6*

LOVE AND KINDNESS

345 I would show love to everyone I know who is younger than me. They would show love to someone else, and it would spread around the world.

Megan N., *Grade 6*

346 I would tell people not to judge people by the color of their skin, but by what is inside.

Viviana L., *Grade 8*

347 You can say "please," and "thank you," and "I'm sorry."

Ev K., *Kindergarten*

348 We could make valentine cards and pass them out all year long, so no one gets left out.

José C., *Grade 3*

349 I can make a joke book for someone who is feeling sad or sick, and then when they don't need it anymore they can give it to someone else.

Joseph R., *Grade 5*

350 I can make a difference by teaching people about the golden rule, "Do unto others as you would have them do unto you."

Kimberly M., *Grade 9*

351 The first thing I could do is have a smile and a "hi" for every person I see.

Christina B., *Grade 5*

352 Generosity and understanding people's differences is something all of us could do to make the world a better place for everybody.

Maria B., *Grade 9*

353 I wish I had the capabilities to make people's skin clear so they would know we have the same organs and blood and we are but one race: human.

Christina C., *Grade 9*

354 I'll treat others how they want to be treated.

Colby L., *Grade 1*

355 One thing we can do to make the world a better place is just to exercise those smiling muscles and say "hi" to everyone you meet.

Heather C., *Grade 9*

356 I will love everyone as they are.

Tiffiny B., *Grade 7*

357 I think we can start to make the world a better place by being patient with each other. When we are impatient, we tend to lose our temper and we hurt each other physically and mentally.

Marie A., *Grade 9*

358 I will pay a compliment to someone every day!

April B., *Grade 6*

359 I will share all my toys with others.

Shawna B., *Grade 1*

360 I would stop criticizing people I don't like.

Lisa M., *Grade 7*

361 I will use my imagination to make the world a better place by drawing pictures for everybody.

Gwen H., *Grade 1*

362 I can make the world a better place by treating people with respect and equality.

Carissa R., *Grade 6*

363 I could make a difference simply by being kind to people, and standing up for the kid who everyone else picks on.

Elizabeth S., *Grade 8*

364 I will do my best to make the world a better place by giving compliments to people. Every day I will say something nice to or about someone to enhance their self-image and brighten their day.

Eric D., *Grade 8*

365 I will use my color markers to make the world beautiful.

Fred A., *Kindergarten*

Here are two ideas from three special kids who have already made a notable contribution to our world, and who plan on keeping up the good work in the new millennium!

★ I would like to find more dinosaurs. My new dinosaur, Zuniceratops Christopheri, lived during a greenhouse world when the sea level was much higher. Studying dinosaurs and their habitats can give us clues about what may happen in our world's future.

Christopher J. Wolfe, *9-year-old co-discoverer of the oldest horned Ceratopsian dinosaur in the world.*

★ Don't be afraid of being lop-sided; devote yourself.

Jason Robert and Erik Engstrom, *17-year-old friends who published their own book,* The Lab Puzzle Book.